How does a telephone work?

DISNEY BOOKS BY MAIL

DK Direct Limited

Managing Art Editor Eljay Crompton
Senior Editor Rosemary McCormick
Writer John Farndon
Illustrators The Alvin White Studios and Richard Manning
Designers Wayne Blades, Veneta Bullen, Richard Clemson,
Sarah Goodwin, Diane Klein, Sonia Whillock

Photo images on page 19 are reproduced courtesy of
Kobal Collection © Lucas Films/Paramount/United Artists

Contents

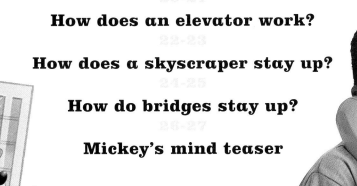

How does electricity get in the house?

Electricity is made in buildings called power stations and comes through wires to your home. Smaller wires inside the walls and under the floor take it around the house to openings in the wall called power outlets. Electrical things, like televisions, can only use the electricity when they are plugged into a power outlet. NEVER touch a power outlet.

High power

Power lines are held safely above the ground, away from people and animals, by tall metal towers called pylons.

Wave power

Some people want to use the power of waves to run the generators that make electricity.

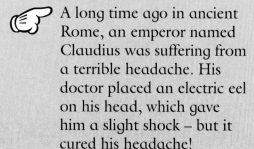

Zappy electricity facts

A long time ago in ancient Rome, an emperor named Claudius was suffering from a terrible headache. His doctor placed an electric eel on his head, which gave him a slight shock – but it cured his headache!

Where does the water in the faucet come from?

It usually comes through pipes from a big lake called a reservoir. On the way to your house, though, it is made clean and safe to drink. Then it gets pumped through big underground pipes called mains. There is a main under your road that supplies water to all the houses and buildings nearby.

8

Splish, splash
What can fall on water without getting wet?
A shadow.

High, low
Big tanks high above the ground called water towers hold lots of water for drinking. They are up high so when you turn on the water in the sink it will pour out whenever you need it.

Holding water up
Reservoirs are sometimes made by building a big wall, called a dam, across a river. The river then slowly fills up the valley behind the dam.

Drip, drop facts

☞ Years ago, people used to collect water from the nearest river and carry it to their homes in buckets.

☞ Every day, the people in New York City use 1.5 billion gallons of water. That's enough to fill 23,000 swimming pools.

Where does the food in the supermarket come from?

All the food in the supermarket comes from a plant or an animal. Hamburger and steak come from cows. Bread is made with the seeds of wheat and other grains, ground into flour. But the food we buy hardly ever looks the way it did on the farm. Before it reaches the store it is often packaged or processed (changed) in factories to make it easier to carry, or nicer to look at.

Staying cool

To stay fresh and good for eating, food is often frozen. Fruit, fish, and meat brought from other countries are often shipped here in special refrigerator ships, trains or trucks.

Food for thought
"Waiter, there's a fly in my soup."
**"Don't worry, Sir, that spider on
your bread will catch it."**

Label game
Next time you go to
the supermarket, see
if you can guess
which plant or
animal the food
came from. Look
for clues on
the label.

Eat up facts

☞ In ancient Rome, favorite
dishes at banquets were –
camels' heels, larks'
tongues and humming
birds in walnut shells.

☞ Food can be a good
weapon, too. In the 17th
century, a ship was saved
from pirates when a
sailor greased its sides
with butter. This stopped
the pirates from climbing
aboard.

11

Where does all our garbage go?

Once, all our garbage was taken to huge pits called landfills. But today landfills are filling up. Also, if we keep throwing away old bottles, boxes, and cans we may soon have nothing to make new ones with! Now anything made of glass, metal or paper can be sent off to be made new. This is called recycling. Only things that can't be recycled should go into landfill pits.

12

Don't waste a thing!
This house in California may look a little odd, but it's very special. It was made out of recycled materials such as bottles and scrap metal.

Metal mouth

The garbage collector empties your trashcan into the garbage truck. The truck has powerful metal jaws that crunch up the garbage so it takes up less space.

Great garbage facts

Most paper is made from trees. If it is recycled, fewer trees need to be cut down. Recycled paper is used in everything from grocery bags to newspapers.

Where do newspapers come from?

When the newspaper is delivered to your door every day, it's because people were up all night getting it there. First the stories are written in the newspaper office. Then thousands of copies are printed and rushed to newspaper-sellers to deliver to homes and newsstands in your town.

14

Hot off the presses
Newspapers are printed on huge machines called printing presses. Hundreds of rolls of paper are printed with stories and pictures.

Where's my dog?
Boy: "I've lost my dog."
Friend: "Why don't you put an advertisement in the newspaper?"
Boy: "Don't be silly, dogs can't read."

Newspaper facts

☞ One tree provides enough paper for 400 newspapers.

☞ Paper can also be made from seaweed, rags, seeds, reeds, and grass.

How does a letter get from you to me?

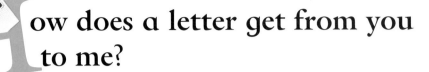

If you want to send a letter to someone, you can put it through the slot at the post office. Inside there are special boxes for the different places a letter might go. For letters going far away, each box is put on a plane and flown off to the right place. Then your letter is given to a mail carrier to be delivered to the right home. Don't forget to put a stamp on the envelope!

16

In the box
You can also drop your letters in a mail box. A mail carrier will collect all the letters and take them to the post office for you.

U.S.MAIL

Zipped up

Every address in the country has its own number, called a zip code. The post office has special machines that read the zip code and send the letter to the correct place.

Pop it in the mail facts

☞ Before stamps were invented, people had to give the mail carrier the money in order to receive their mail.

☞ A mail carrier's life is not always a happy one. Each year, thousands of mail carriers report that they have been bitten by dogs. Woof, woof!

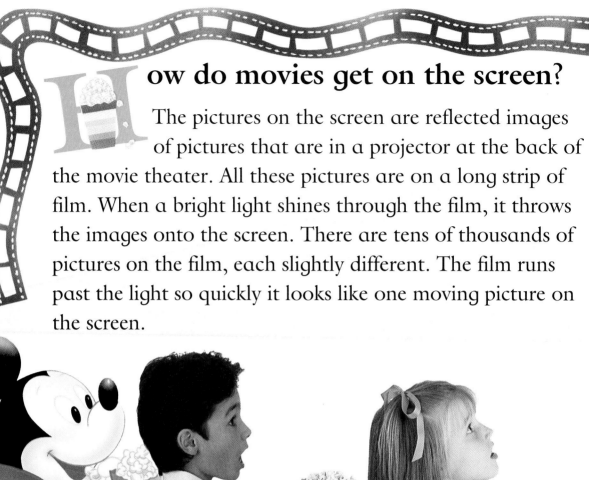

How do movies get on the screen?

The pictures on the screen are reflected images of pictures that are in a projector at the back of the movie theater. All these pictures are on a long strip of film. When a bright light shines through the film, it throws the images onto the screen. There are tens of thousands of pictures on the film, each slightly different. The film runs past the light so quickly it looks like one moving picture on the screen.

Fast pictures!
Can you
imagine – 24
pictures pass
in front of the
projector light
every second.

Sounds great!
The movie's sound is
usually recorded at the
same time as the actors are
being filmed. Microphones
are used to pick up the
sound of their voices. The
sound and the pictures are
all on the same piece of
film.

Making movies

☞ Early movies were in
black and white and they
didn't have sound.

☞ Color movies were first
made in 1941.

☞ Between 1959 and 1960,
"smelly" movies were
popular. Different smells
were piped to where the
audience were seated so
they could smell the
scenes in the film!

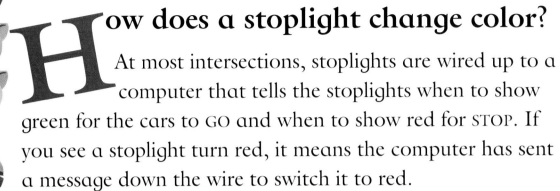

How does a stoplight change color?

At most intersections, stoplights are wired up to a computer that tells the stoplights when to show green for the cars to GO and when to show red for STOP. If you see a stoplight turn red, it means the computer has sent a message down the wire to switch it to red.

Lunch time!
What did the traffic officer have in his sandwich?
Traffic jam!

Traffic control

There are sometimes special pads under the road to count the cars that pass over. The computer can match the time stoplights stay green to the number of cars passing by.

Traffic officer

When stoplights break down, a police officer tells the cars when to stop. When the officer holds one hand up toward you, it means – STOP!

21

Flashing stoplight facts

☞ Stoplight colors are always in the same order. Red is always on the top and green is always on the bottom.

☞ Can you imagine – three million cars drive into New York City every day.

How does an elevator work?

Elevators are like small rooms carrying you up and down inside a long narrow space called an elevator shaft. Either at the top, or bottom, of the elevator shaft is a powerful motor. When you press the elevator button to go up, the motor turns a wheel to wind up a long steel wire that pulls the elevator up the shaft.

Top to bottom facts

A man named Elisha Otis worked in a factory making large, heavy beds. To save the workers from having to carry them up and down stairs, he built elevators big enough to do it!

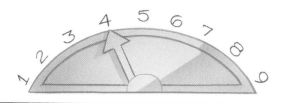

Staying up

If the wire breaks, springs or rollers on top of the elevator jam against each side of the shaft to keep it from falling.

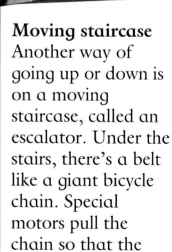

Moving staircase

Another way of going up or down is on a moving staircase, called an escalator. Under the stairs, there's a belt like a giant bicycle chain. Special motors pull the chain so that the stairs go around.

How does a skyscraper stay up?

It has foundations and a strong steel frame. A skyscraper may look all glass and concrete, but inside there is a steel frame that holds the building together. Skyscrapers are built on sturdy foundations. These are made by setting concrete and steel into holes dug deep in the ground.

Tall story
The world's tallest building is the Sears Tower in Chicago. It's 1,454 feet tall. That's about as big as 35 houses stacked on top of each other.

Very tall facts

☞ Before skyscrapers, tall buildings were made of stone.

☞ In 1945, a B25 bomber crashed into the 79th floor of the Empire State Building in New York. A few columns and beams were bent, but the main structure of the building was so strong, amazingly, it was undamaged.

Going up
Builders put up a skyscraper by adding steel piece by piece, then covering them in concrete.

How do bridges stay up?

There are many ways. The simplest way to build a bridge is to place a piece of wood over a stream. But the biggest bridges, that cross wide rivers, are usually "suspension" bridges. A suspension bridge has a tower at either end, and may have other towers in the middle. Suspension simply means hanging. The roadway, where the cars go, hangs from the towers on metal cables.

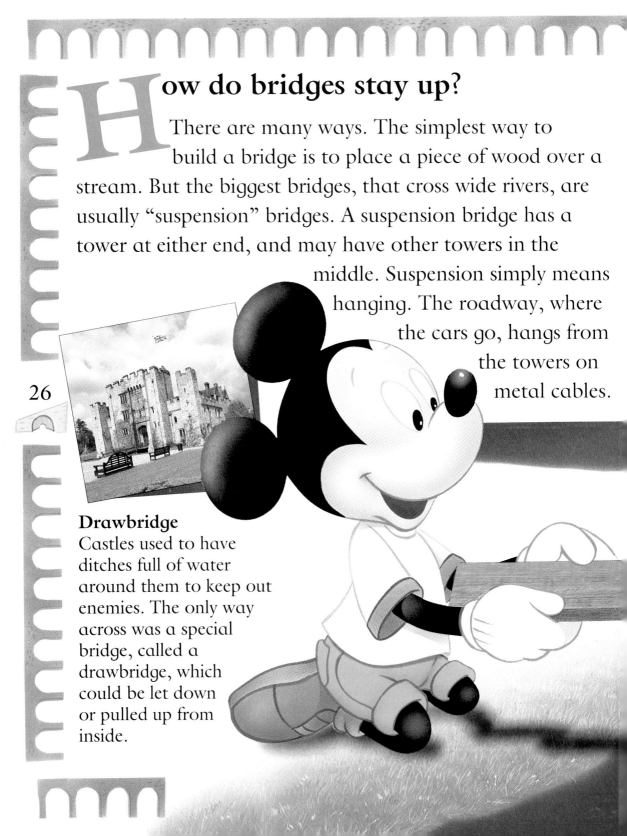

Drawbridge
Castles used to have ditches full of water around them to keep out enemies. The only way across was a special bridge, called a drawbridge, which could be let down or pulled up from inside.

Golden Gate

The Golden Gate Bridge in San Francisco is one of the world's longest suspension bridges. Its towers are almost a mile apart.

Bridge facts

The earliest suspension bridges were made from ropes or twisted plants called creepers.

Hundreds of years ago, people used to build houses on bridges.

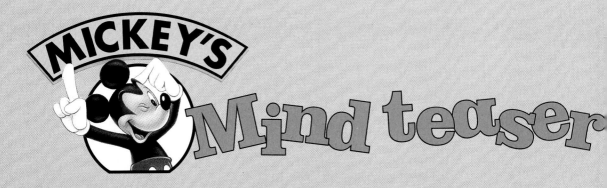

Do you know what job each person does?

1. Newspaper delivery person; 2. Elevator operator; 3. Mail carrier; 4. Garbage collector; 5. Check-out person.